Passion to Profit

A Homeschool Parent's Guide
to Creating an Education Business

Dr. Annise Mabry

Passion to Profit

A Homeschool Parent's Guide
to Creating an Education Business

Dr. Annise Mabry

PASSION TO PROFIT

A Homeschool Parent's Guide to Creating an Education Business

Dr. Annise Mabry

Copyright © 2025 by The Dr. Annise Mabry Foundation Inc

FIRST EDITION
ISBN 979-8-9914876-3-4

Dedication

To the woman I had to become to write this book,

the one who turned breakdowns into breakthroughs, grief into grit, and passion into purpose. You were forged in fire, and every page of this book is your victory cry.

To the original Tiers Free families,

thank you for saying yes when the world told you no. You were the blueprint before there was a roadmap, the foundation before there was a structure. We built this together.

To every student and family who dared to believe,

you turned this dream into a movement. Your faith, your resilience, and your refusal to give up have given this work its heartbeat.

To every mother who dared to dream out loud.

This is for the ones who turned kitchen tables into boardrooms, pain into purpose, and passion into power.

This book is your answer.

May it be your blueprint, your mirror, and your permission slip.

Never forget—your passion is profitable.

About The Author

Dr. Annise Mabry is a nationally recognized edupreneur, strategist, and community impact architect. Long before edupreneurship became a buzzword, Dr. Mabry was developing a homeschool-based business model that defied conventional thinking and changed the lives of thousands in the process.

As the founder of The Dr. Annise Mabry Foundation and Tiers Free Academy, she pioneered a trauma-informed, diploma-granting homeschool cooperative that has served over 6,000 families and issued more than 1,000 high school diplomas to students who were left behind by traditional education systems.

A trusted expert in grant writing and sustainable program development, Dr. Mabry has secured millions of dollars in federal, state, corporate, and foundation-level grants to fund education, mental health, and workforce programs in rural communities. Her unique ability to merge community needs with entrepreneurial innovation has positioned her as a leading voice in the edupreneurship movement.

Today, she mentors emerging edupreneurs, nonprofit leaders, and grassroots changemakers by helping them turn their passion into profitable, community-rooted solutions.

TABLE OF CONTENTS

 # Prologue

When I first embarked on the journey of homeschooling, it wasn't because I wanted to—it was because I had to. My children were struggling, and I realized the traditional education system couldn't meet their needs. As their mother, I was their last line of defense, and I knew I had to figure it out, one step at a time.

What started as a necessity soon became something more. It became a calling. I didn't just want to homeschool my children—I wanted to reimagine what education could look like. I saw potential in personalized learning and flexibility, and I wanted to create a path that empowered not only my family but also others who felt left behind by the system.

But let me tell you, the journey wasn't easy. There were moments when I questioned if I was doing the right thing. There were sleepless nights, endless challenges, and plenty of people who doubted me. Yet, through it all, one thing kept me going: the belief that education has the power to change lives.

This book is more than a guide—it's a testament to what's possible when you follow your passion and step out in faith. It's a collection of lessons I've learned, strategies that worked for me, and stories from families and students who found hope and success through homeschooling. My goal is simple: to inspire you to dream bigger, think creatively, and take bold steps toward building something extraordinary.

If you are here, it means you're ready to take your passion for homeschooling and turn it into something that impacts lives far beyond your own. Whether you're starting a homeschool business, launching a cooperative, or simply looking to make your educational journey more fulfilling, this book will guide you every step of the way.

So, let's talk about how you can transform your passion into profit, your challenges into opportunities, and your dreams into a legacy. Grab a cup of coffee, pull up a chair, and together, we'll explore how to not only teach, but to truly transform lives. Welcome to the journey. Let's get started.

Passion to Profit

A Homeschool Parent's Guide
to Creating an Education Business

Dr. Annise Mabry

 # Chapter 1

INTRODUCTION TO PASSION AND PROFIT

UNDERSTANDING THE HOMESCHOOL LANDSCAPE

When I started homeschooling in 2012, I didn't have the luxury of surveying the landscape to analyze what I was doing; I had to jump in feet first because my children were struggling. I was the only reliable resource they had, and as their mother, it was my job to save them.

The homeschool landscape has evolved significantly over the last few decades, transforming from a niche educational choice into a mainstream option embraced by millions of families. This shift is largely driven by a growing recognition of the benefits of personalized education, flexibility in learning environments, and a desire for greater parental involvement in children's academic journeys. As a homeschool parent, it is vital to familiarize yourself with the diverse elements that shape this landscape, as they can influence both your educational approach and potential business opportunities.

What I wish traditional educators understood about homeschooling is how different it is. Traditional education is like a straight road with clear rules and guardrails—everything runs through accreditation. Homeschooling, though? It's a whole other world. Over the years, it's gone from being a quirky niche to a mainstream choice for millions of families. Why? Because it offers things traditional schools often can't: personalized learning, flexibility, and a chance for parents to take the lead in their kids' education.

If you're a homeschooling parent, it's so important to get a feel for this ever-changing landscape. Not only will it help you make the most of your homeschooling journey, but you might also discover some unexpected opportunities along the way. Homeschooling is not just a backup plan—it is a way to rethink how we approach learning altogether.

One key aspect of the homeschool landscape is the variety of educational philosophies and methodologies available. From classical education and Montessori to unschooling and eclectic approaches, each philosophy offers unique benefits and challenges. Understanding these distinctions can help you identify the most suitable method for your family's learning style and values. Additionally, as you consider turning your passion for homeschooling into a profitable business, recognizing the prevalent philosophies can guide you in developing your niche educational products or services that resonate with other homeschool families. It's important to realize that you don't need to be everything to every homeschool family—only those families that you want to fit into your niche.

When I first launched Tiers Free Homeschool Cooperative, I had a clear vision of who I wanted to serve: struggling high school students and their families. It wasn't that I didn't want to help younger students, but I had the experience to understand that elementary-aged students require a lot of adult support. The parents of these younger children were often in two camps—either hovering so much that the children didn't get the chance to fail and learn from their mistakes, or they were pushing for such high levels of independence that the expectations were simply too unrealistic for the child's age. These dynamics didn't align with the model I wanted to create. My area of interest at the time was with high school students, and that became my niche audience.

In 2020, after several years of successfully operating Tiers Free Homeschool Cooperative, we expanded to serve grades K-12, but my initial focus was very much on high school. When I eventually ventured into the elementary and middle school homeschool space, I had a tremendous advantage. By building the program from the high school level down, I was able to address the skills gaps that I had seen firsthand in my high school students. This approach allowed me to design a curriculum that was intentional and strategic, ensuring that younger students would have a strong foundation and avoid many of the struggles I had witnessed at the high school level.

Another important factor is the legal framework surrounding homeschooling. Each state or country has its own regulations, from notification requirements to curriculum choices and assessment methods. Familiarizing yourself with these laws is crucial not only to ensure compliance but also to identify potential gaps in the market where your business could thrive. For instance, if you discover that many parents in your area struggle with record-keeping or understanding assessment requirements, you could create resources or support services tailored to those needs.

The community aspect of homeschooling plays a pivotal role in shaping the landscape. Homeschooling often involves forming cooperative groups, co-ops, or support networks where families share resources, organize joint activities, and provide socialization opportunities for their children. Engaging with these communities can be incredibly beneficial for your educational journey and can also serve as a fertile ground for business ideas. By connecting with other homeschool families, you can gain insights into their needs, preferences, and challenges, allowing you to tailor your offerings to better serve them.

In recent years, the increasing integration of technology into education has transformed the homeschool landscape, opening up new avenues for both learning and business. Online courses, interactive apps, and virtual tutoring services are just a few examples of how technology can enhance the homeschooling experience. As you navigate this landscape, consider how you can leverage technology to create innovative products or services that meet the evolving needs of homeschool families. By staying informed about trends and tools in the educational technology sector, you can position your business to thrive in this dynamic environment.

THE RISE OF EDUCATION ENTREPRENEURSHIP

The landscape of education is undergoing a significant transformation, with traditional models giving way to innovative approaches that cater to diverse learning needs. Among these changes, the rise of education entrepreneurship is particularly noteworthy. This trend is not merely a reaction to the challenges faced by conventional educational systems; it represents a fundamental shift in how knowledge is delivered and consumed. For homeschool parents, this offers a unique opportunity to turn their passion for education into a profitable business, creating tailored learning experiences that resonate with today's learners. Education entrepreneurship encompasses a broad spectrum of initiatives, from online courses and tutoring services to educational products and resources. Many homeschool parents are uniquely positioned to identify gaps in the market due to their firsthand experience with traditional educational limitations. They possess valuable insights into what children need to thrive academically and emotionally. As they navigate their homeschooling journeys, these parents often develop innovative curricula, learning tools, and community resources that can be expanded into viable business ventures. This shift not only benefits their own families but also offers solutions to others seeking effective educational alternatives.

The increasing demand for personalized education solutions has fueled the growth of education entrepreneurship. With the rise of technology and online platforms, homeschool parents can reach a global audience, sharing their expertise in specialized subjects or unique teaching methods. This accessibility allows them to create scalable businesses that go beyond local markets. Parents can develop online courses, write e-books, or even launch subscription-based learning platforms.

The success stories of those who have ventured into this realm serve as inspiration, demonstrating that passion for education can translate into financial sustainability.

Moreover, the sense of community among homeschooling families can be a powerful asset for education entrepreneurs. By leveraging social media and networking opportunities, parents can connect with like-minded individuals who share their vision. This camaraderie not only provides emotional support but also opens doors to collaboration. Joint ventures, co-op programs, and shared resources can enhance the educational offerings available to families, creating a vibrant ecosystem that benefits everyone involved. Such collaborations can also increase visibility, allowing education entrepreneurs to establish their brands and reach broader audiences.

The rise of education entrepreneurship represents a promising avenue for homeschool parents eager to transform their passion for education into profitable ventures. By recognizing the potential for innovation within the educational landscape, these parents can create meaningful change while achieving financial independence. As they embark on this journey, they contribute not only to their own families' success but also to the broader movement toward personalized, engaging, and effective education solutions. Embracing this entrepreneurial spirit can lead to fulfilling careers that align with their values and priorities, ultimately enriching the lives of countless learners.

IDENTIFYING YOUR PASSION

One way to pinpoint your passion is to explore the challenges you have faced as a homeschool parent. Reflect on the hurdles that you have navigated and how they might translate into business opportunities. For instance, if you found it difficult to source engaging educational resources, consider creating a platform that connects parents with curated materials. When I started homeschooling, it was out of sheer necessity. It took me a few years to first heal from the trauma that came from having to homeschool because we were out of options in public and private school.

It's important to understand that passion doesn't always have to start at the beginning. It can emerge as you realize the potential not only to teach your children but also to grow personally and professionally by building a business that creates financial independence. Whether homeschooling is a necessity, a choice, or a preference, the act of turning it into a successful venture can inspire a sense of fulfillment and pride.

This sense of purpose can evolve into a true passion when you reflect on what aspects of homeschooling excite you most. Do you love designing creative lesson plans, or do you find joy in the one-on-one connections with your children? Recognizing your strengths and interests will help guide you toward a business model that feels authentic, sustainable, and deeply rewarding.

When I embarked on the journey to identify my passion, I had one mantra: "Do what makes you happy." For me, this meant that if something in my homeschool journey with my children didn't bring me immediate joy, I started to outsource it. I outsourced so much of my son's homeschooling that we were going to a different homeschool cooperative or a different tutor daily. I was a much better mom and a more effective learning facilitator for him when I was the secondary educator rather than the primary educator.

Conducting a personal inventory is a great first step to finding what makes you happy. What makes you happy is your passion. My happy was in designing curriculum and deep diving into the nuances of homeschool law. Consider your experiences, skills, and the subjects or activities you are most passionate about. Make a list of the aspects of homeschooling that energize you and those that you excel in. This could range from curriculum development to hands-on learning experiences, or even community engagement. The more specific you can be, the clearer your path will become. Remember, your passion should align with your values and interests, ensuring that your business remains a source of fulfillment rather than stress.

Engaging with your homeschool community can also provide valuable insights into your passion. Discussing your journey with other homeschool parents can reveal shared interests and potential business ideas. Attend local homeschooling events or join online forums to gather feedback on what resonates with others. Often, the conversations you have with fellow parents can illuminate aspects of your experience that you may not have considered. By understanding the needs and desires of your community, you can tailor your business to address those gaps, making it more relevant and appealing.

Alternatively, if you have developed unique teaching strategies that have worked well for your family, you could offer workshops or online courses to share your expertise. By transforming your challenges into solutions, you not only identify your passion but also create a service that can genuinely help others.

Tiers Free Homeschool Cooperative was born out of necessity to provide academic instruction to my own children. Tiers Free Academy grew out of an experiment to issue a homeschool high school diploma to my neighbor's daughter. Never underestimate the power of experimentation. Without my own experience of building something to educate my own children, I wouldn't have had the knowledge that I needed to issue a homeschool high school diploma to my neighbor's daughter.

Sometimes, the best way to discover your passion is to try different avenues within the homeschooling sphere. Start small by offering tutoring services, creating educational materials, or hosting workshops. As you gain experience, pay attention to what you enjoy most and where you see the most engagement from your audience. This iterative process will help you refine your focus and eventually lead you to a business model that not only aligns with your passion but also has the potential for profitability. Embrace the journey of exploration, and allow your passion to evolve as you build your education business.

Chapter 2

FINDING YOUR NICHE

ASSESSING YOUR SKILLS AND INTERESTS

As a homeschool parent, you bring unique experiences and perspectives to the table—insights that have the potential to make a real difference in the educational world. By reflecting on what you enjoy and where you excel, you can find a niche that feels authentic and meaningful. Beyond creating something that works for others, you will be building a business that fulfills your creative and personal goals while making a positive impact. Assessing your skills and interests is a critical first step in transforming your passion for homeschooling into a profitable business.

Sometimes, what begins as an obligation or a simple preference—just another aspect of parenting—can transform into something extraordinary. Homeschooling, for instance, might feel like a duty you've taken on for your child's benefit, a choice driven by necessity or convenience. But hidden within that responsibility lies the potential for something more: a journey of discovery, growth, and even passion. You may not yet realize the immense joy and fulfillment waiting on the other side of this commitment. As you navigate the challenges and triumphs of teaching your child, you may uncover talents and interests you never knew you had. The act of creating, problem-solving, and building something meaningful—a thriving homeschool environment or even a business—can awaken a deeper purpose and pride within you. What once felt like a burden can become a source of incredible satisfaction and success, proving that sometimes our greatest joys are hidden in the opportunities we least expect. A comprehensive inventory of your skills will provide a solid foundation for determining how they can be translated into a business model.

Next, delve into your interests outside of homeschooling. Do you have a passion for arts and crafts, science experiments, or technology? Exploring these interests can help you identify how they can be integrated into your educational offerings. For instance, if you love gardening, you could develop a curriculum or workshop focused on outdoor education. Engaging with your personal interests can spark creativity and innovation, allowing you to create unique educational products or services that stand out in the market. This alignment of personal passion with professional opportunities is essential for sustained motivation and success.

Another important aspect of assessing your skills and interests is understanding your target audience. What are the needs and challenges faced by other homeschool parents? What resources do they seek? What gaps exist in the current market? When I started my homeschool cooperative as a Facebook group, it was because there was a gap in homeschool groups for families with children who learned differently.

As a homeschool parent, you are already in the homeschool spaces, so start conducting surveys, joining online forums, or participating in local homeschooling events beyond your regular homeschool group. This will allow you to gather insights into what potential customers are looking for. This research will not only help you refine your business idea but also ensure that your offerings are relevant and valuable to your audience. Aligning your skills and interests with the needs of others is a powerful strategy for establishing a successful education business.

Once you've redefined your business idea, it's time to define your mission and vision. It's essential to create a personal mission statement that encapsulates your vision for your business. This statement should reflect your core values, the impact you wish to make in the homeschooling community, and how your skills and interests will play a role in achieving that vision. As you navigate the challenges of starting a business, a clear mission will serve as a guiding principle and will help you stay focused on your objectives. By thoroughly assessing your skills and interests, you can confidently move forward in your journey from passion to profit.

RESEARCHING MARKET DEMANDS

If you're new to both homeschooling and starting a business, the idea of creating a homeschool education business can feel overwhelming. However, researching market demands is a critical first step that will set you up for success. Understanding what other homeschooling parents need and want will not only help you design services and products that resonate with your audience but also ensure your business fills a meaningful gap in the market.

Begin by immersing yourself in the homeschooling community. This could be through online forums, social media groups, or local homeschooling networks. Engage in conversations to uncover the common challenges parents face, such as finding affordable resources, addressing learning gaps, or navigating specific educational subjects. Listen for insights on what tools or support they wish existed. By actively participating in these spaces, you can identify unmet needs and position your business as the solution to those problems.

Next, consider directly reaching out to your potential customers. This can be done through surveys or casual interviews with homeschooling parents in your area or online groups. Ask them about their pain points, the resources they currently rely on, and the features they feel are missing from existing offerings. This type of feedback not only helps you refine your business idea but also builds trust and credibility within your community—a crucial factor when starting a new venture.

Understanding your competition is another important aspect of market research. Look at businesses that cater to homeschooling families to analyze their strengths, weaknesses, and pricing strategies. What services do they offer that are popular? What gaps do they leave unaddressed? By learning from their successes and shortcomings, you can tailor your business to stand out and meet the needs they may have overlooked.

Finally, stay informed about broader trends in education and homeschooling. Changes in policies, new technology, or shifting societal attitudes toward homeschooling can create opportunities for innovative business ideas. Attend webinars, follow industry blogs, and join professional networks to stay ahead of the curve.

By taking the time to research market demands, you'll not only gain a clearer picture of your audience but also build a strong foundation for a business that turns your homeschooling journey into a rewarding and sustainable venture.

CREATING A UNIQUE VALUE PROPOSITION (UVP)

When starting your homeschool education business, crafting a Unique Value Proposition (UVP) is key to standing out in a competitive market. A UVP explains why your business is special and how it uniquely meets the needs of homeschool families. This clarity helps attract customers and fosters trust, making it essential for a successful start.

Begin by focusing on the specific problems or desires of other homeschool parents. Do they need creative curriculum options, extra help with specific subjects, or a sense of community? Identifying these needs lets you offer solutions that feel personal and relevant. For example, if parents in your area struggle to find STEM resources, you could specialize in providing hands-on science kits or online tutoring tailored to those subjects.

Your UVP should also reflect what makes *you* unique. What have you learned from your homeschooling experience? Have you developed strategies to manage challenging behaviors or created engaging methods for teaching tough topics? Your personal story is often the most compelling part of your business. Highlighting these details not only differentiates your offerings but also builds credibility as someone who truly understands the homeschooling journey.

Once you have a clear idea of your audience's needs and your distinct strengths, create a UVP that is concise, memorable, and customer-focused. For instance, if your focus is on helping parents of struggling readers, your UVP could be: "Empowering homeschool families with tailored tools to help struggling readers thrive academically and emotionally."

Finally, test your UVP. Share it with peers, potential customers, or members of homeschooling groups to see how it resonates. Their feedback will help refine your message, ensuring it speaks directly to your audience while staying true to your vision.

By crafting a UVP that combines your personal expertise with solutions to real challenges, you set the stage for a thriving homeschool business that serves families in a meaningful and impactful way.

 **Chapter 3**

CREATING A BUSINESS PLAN

DEFINING YOUR BUSINESS MODEL

Starting your homeschool education business begins with defining your business model. This means deciding how your business will operate, what services or products you'll offer, and how you'll make money. Think of it as your roadmap to success.

Start by asking yourself: what do you love about homeschooling, and what are you good at? Your skills and experiences as a homeschool parent can guide you. These strengths can form the foundation of your business.

Next, consider how to earn money. Will you charge for one-on-one tutoring, sell ready-made lesson plans, or host online workshops? Think about offering a mix of services, such as a subscription plan for resources alongside occasional live classes. A variety of options can make your business more sustainable.

When I first started, defining my business model was one of the hardest parts because I didn't have a clear framework to follow. It took me years to fully understand the actual costs of taking just one high school student through the diploma program. When you're creating your business model, focus on building for today while ensuring that your foundation is sustainable for the future.

The global pandemic of 2020 serves as a powerful reminder of why sustainability is crucial. Many homeschool cooperatives that had been thriving for decades were forced to close permanently because their models weren't designed to withstand sudden change. In contrast, my online homeschool cooperative was built with scalability and adaptability in mind, which allowed us to step in and fill the gap left by those closures. Being prepared for unexpected challenges can make the difference between surviving and thriving in the long term.

Remember to listen to feedback and adjust as you go. The homeschooling world changes quickly, so stay flexible and keep your business aligned with what families need most.

SETTING GOALS AND OBJECTIVES

Setting clear goals is an important first step when starting your business. Goals help you focus and measure progress. Start with your big-picture vision: what do you want your business to achieve? For example, do you want to help children master math or guide parents through the challenges of homeschooling?

Break your vision into smaller, actionable steps. If your goal is to offer online courses, start with creating one course. Once you see success, expand your offerings. Use SMART goals—specific, measurable, achievable, relevant, and time-bound—to make sure your steps are clear and doable.

Check in on your goals regularly. Are they still realistic? Do they need adjusting? Revisiting your goals ensures you're always moving in the right direction. And don't forget to celebrate small wins—they keep you motivated!

BUDGETING FOR YOUR BUSINESS

Budgeting may sound intimidating, but it's simply about planning how to spend your money wisely. Start by listing your startup costs. These might include things like a website, teaching supplies, or marketing materials.

Don't forget about ongoing costs, such as subscriptions for tools or software you'll need.

Next, think about how you'll make money. Will parents pay for courses, buy lesson plans, or subscribe to your services? Research what other homeschool businesses charge to get an idea of fair pricing. Plan for different income scenarios—best case, average, and worst case—so you're ready for anything.

Finally, review your budget often. As your business grows, your expenses and income will change. Staying flexible helps you adapt and make the most of new opportunities.

By breaking things down into clear steps, you can build a homeschool business that feels manageable, rewarding, and successful.

 **Chapter 4**

BUILDING YOUR BRAND

CRAFTING A STRONG BRAND IDENTITY

As a homeschool parent launching a business, crafting a strong brand identity is essential for standing out in a competitive market. Your brand identity is more than a name or logo—it's the heart of your business, encapsulating your mission, values, and the unique value you bring to the homeschooling community. A well-defined brand builds trust and fosters connection with your audience, turning your passion for education into a thriving enterprise.

DEFINING YOUR MISSION AND VALUES

The first step in creating your brand identity is clarifying your mission and values. Why are you passionate about homeschooling, and what drives your desire to share your knowledge? For example, Tiers Free Homeschool Cooperative focuses on providing trauma-informed, customized educational solutions for at-risk students. Its mission isn't just about awarding diplomas—it's about giving students a second chance and helping families regain hope.

Your mission should reflect what makes your approach unique while aligning with the needs of your target audience. Be authentic and specific. For instance, if your goal is to support parents of struggling readers, center your brand around providing solutions that empower families and foster academic confidence.

CREATING A VISUAL IDENTITY

Your visual identity communicates your brand at a glance. This includes your logo, color scheme, typography, and overall design aesthetic. These elements should align with your mission and values while appealing to your audience. For a brand like Tiers Free, warm, inviting colors and imagery that highlights diverse learners help convey inclusivity and support.

If your focus is innovation, consider dynamic designs and modern fonts. For a more nurturing approach, opt for soft colors and organic visuals. Whatever direction you choose, consistency across your website, social media, and print materials strengthens brand recognition.

SHARING YOUR STORY

Storytelling is a powerful way to connect with your audience. Share your journey as a homeschool parent, the challenges you've faced, and the lessons you've learned. For example, Tiers Free often highlights stories of students overcoming adversity, emphasizing the cooperative's role in transforming lives.

Your story humanizes your brand and establishes credibility. Use blog posts, webinars, or social media to share these narratives. Authentic, consistent messaging builds trust and positions you as a relatable expert within the homeschooling community.

BUILDING COMMUNITY CONNECTIONS

A strong brand doesn't just provide services—it creates a community. Engage with your audience through social media, forums, and local events. Encourage feedback and foster conversations that deepen connections. Tiers Free built its success not only by offering solutions but also by creating a space where families feel heard and supported.

By combining a clear mission, a cohesive visual identity, and meaningful storytelling, you can craft a brand that resonates deeply with homeschooling families. Just like Tiers Free Homeschool Cooperative, your business can become a trusted resource and a symbol of support and success in the homeschooling community.

DEVELOPING YOUR ONLINE PRESENCE

Developing a robust online presence is essential for homeschool parents looking to transform their passion for education into a profitable business. In today's digital landscape, having a well-defined online identity can help you reach a broader audience, connect with like-minded individuals, and establish yourself as an authority in the homeschooling community. This subchapter will guide you through the key steps to create and enhance your online presence, providing you with the tools needed to effectively share your expertise and attract potential clients.

The first step in developing your online presence is to define your brand. Consider what makes your approach to homeschooling unique and how you want to communicate that to your audience. Your brand encompasses your mission, values, and the specific niche you wish to serve within the homeschooling community. Take the time to craft a clear and compelling brand story that resonates with your target audience. This foundational work will inform your messaging, visual identity, and marketing strategies moving forward.

Next, establishing a professional website is crucial. Your website serves as a central hub for your online activities, where potential clients can learn more about your offerings, access valuable resources, and connect with you. Invest in a user-friendly design that reflects your brand and is easy to navigate. Include essential elements such as a blog, service descriptions, testimonials, and a contact form. Consistently updating your website with fresh content will not only engage visitors but also enhance your search engine visibility, making it easier for others to find you online.

Utilizing social media platforms can significantly amplify your online presence. Choose platforms that align with your target audience's preferences and where your content can thrive, such as Facebook, Instagram, or Pinterest. Share valuable insights, tips, and experiences related to homeschooling, and engage with your followers through comments and discussions. Regularly posting relevant content can help you build a community around your brand and establish trust with your audience. Additionally, consider joining or creating online groups focused on homeschooling to further connect with potential clients and showcase your expertise.

Lastly, identifying and implementing effective marketing strategies will elevate your online presence. Content marketing, such as blogging or creating videos, allows you to share your knowledge and attract an audience organically. Email marketing can also be a powerful tool for nurturing relationships with your audience, providing them with tailored content that aligns with their interests. Collaborating with other educators or influencers in the homeschooling niche can expand your reach and introduce your brand to new potential clients. By strategically combining these efforts, you can create a comprehensive online presence that not only showcases your passion for homeschooling but also drives your business toward profitability.

ESTABLISHING CREDIBILITY AND TRUST

Establishing credibility and trust is a foundational element in transforming your passion for homeschooling into a successful education business. For homeschool parents venturing into the entrepreneurial realm, the importance of being perceived as a reliable source of information and guidance cannot be overstated.

Parents seeking resources for their children are naturally cautious; they want to ensure that the services and products they invest in are worth their time and money. Therefore, building a reputation for expertise and reliability is essential for attracting and retaining clients.

One of the most effective ways to establish credibility is by showcasing your qualifications and experiences. Share your homeschooling journey, including any relevant certifications or training you have completed.

Highlight the successes you have achieved with your own children, such as their academic achievements or social development. Providing testimonials from other parents who have benefited from your guidance can also significantly enhance your credibility. When potential clients see evidence of your expertise and the positive impact you have made, they are more likely to trust you with their own children's education.

In addition to sharing your personal story, creating high-quality, informative content is a powerful strategy for establishing authority in the homeschooling niche. Consider developing a blog, podcast, or video series that addresses common challenges faced by homeschool parents. This content should not only showcase your knowledge but also offer practical solutions and resources. Consistently providing valuable information positions you as a thought leader and builds trust with your audience. As parents engage with your content, they will come to view you as a go-to resource, increasing the likelihood that they will turn to you for additional services.

Networking within the homeschooling community can also play a crucial role in establishing credibility. Attend local homeschooling events, workshops, and online forums to connect with other parents and educators. By actively participating in discussions and sharing your insights, you can build relationships that enhance your reputation. Collaborating with other trusted figures in the homeschooling space, such as co-hosting workshops or contributing to established educational platforms, can further validate your expertise. The more you engage with the community, the more your name will become synonymous with quality and trustworthiness.

Finally, maintaining transparency and integrity in your business practices is vital for fostering long-term trust. Be clear about your offerings, pricing, and any potential limitations of your services. If you make a mistake, acknowledge it and take steps to rectify the situation.

Building trust takes time, but it can be easily lost if clients feel misled or unsupported. By prioritizing honesty and open communication, you demonstrate to your clients that you are genuinely invested in their children's education and well-being.

This commitment not only solidifies your credibility but also encourages clients to recommend your services to others, further expanding your reach within the homeschooling community.

 **Chapter 5**

LEGAL AND FINANCIAL CONSIDERATIONS

CHOOSING THE RIGHT BUSINESS STRUCTURE

Starting your first business as a homeschool parent may feel overwhelming, but choosing the right business structure doesn't have to be. Your business structure affects everything from taxes to liability to how your business operates day-to-day. Let's explore the options and break them down into simple terms to help you choose what works best for your unique situation.

1. SOLE PROPRIETORSHIP

This is the simplest and most common option for new business owners. As a sole proprietor, you and your business are legally the same, meaning there's no formal registration required. This is a great choice if you're testing the waters and want to start small with minimal upfront costs. However, be aware that as a sole proprietor, your personal assets (like your home or savings) could be at risk if your business incurs debt or faces legal challenges.

2. Partnership

If you plan to team up with another homeschool parent or educator, a partnership might be the right choice. This structure allows you to share decision-making and pool resources. However, like a sole proprietorship, both partners are personally liable for the business's debts. To avoid misunderstandings, it's crucial to create a partnership agreement that clearly outlines responsibilities, profit-sharing, and decision-making processes.

3. Limited Liability Company (LLC)

An LLC provides the best of both worlds: flexibility and liability protection. Your personal assets are shielded from business liabilities, and profits are taxed directly on your personal tax return (known as "pass-through taxation"). This structure is ideal for homeschool parents who want to grow their business while keeping things manageable. While there are some setup fees and requirements, the benefits often outweigh the costs, especially if you're planning to reinvest profits into your business.

4. Nonprofit Corporation (501c3)

If your mission is rooted in serving a community or tackling educational inequities, forming a nonprofit corporation might be the best path for you. When I started The Dr. Annise Mabry Foundation, I quickly learned that a nonprofit is still very much a business—it requires the same focus, strategy, and commitment as any for-profit venture. The key difference? Every dollar you earn goes back into fueling your mission, not into an owner's pocket. While the nonprofit model can unlock grants and funding opportunities, it's not an easy road. There are countless misconceptions, from how funding works to what qualifies as a nonprofit activity. But let me tell you, if your heart is set on creating meaningful, lasting community impact, the hard work is worth it. A nonprofit is more than simply an organization; it is a vehicle for change.

5. Corporation

If you're thinking big and plan to seek investors or grow significantly, a corporation might be worth exploring. While it provides the highest level of liability protection, a corporation comes with more regulatory requirements and may not be necessary for most homeschool businesses.

HOW TO DECIDE

The best structure for your business depends on your goals, the level of risk you're comfortable with, and how much time and money you're ready to invest. Start small if you're unsure, and don't hesitate to consult a professional to ensure you're making the right decision for your situation.

UNDERSTANDING TAXES AND LICENSES

Taxes and licenses might seem intimidating at first, but understanding them is essential for running a legal and successful business. Here's what you need to know:

Taxes

- **Self-Employment Tax:** As a business owner, you'll pay Social Security and Medicare taxes for yourself.
- **Income Tax:** This will depend on your total earnings. Keep records of your income to stay prepared for tax season.
- **Sales Tax:** If you sell educational products or services, you may need to collect and remit sales tax to your state.

LICENSING

Depending on your business type, you may need a license. For example, if you're offering tutoring or workshops, check with local and state agencies to ensure compliance. It's better to research and handle these requirements upfront than to face issues later.

STAYING ORGANIZED

Track all your income and expenses carefully. Use accounting software or a simple spreadsheet to stay on top of things, and consider consulting a tax professional to make sure you're on the right path.

 **Chapter 6**

MARKETING YOUR EDUCATION BUSINESS

LEVERAGING SOCIAL MEDIA AND ONLINE MARKETING FOR YOUR HOMESCHOOL BUSINESS

Social media and online marketing are powerful tools for homeschool parents looking to turn their passion for education into a thriving business. These platforms offer a unique opportunity to connect with a broader audience, build meaningful relationships, and grow your brand. Here's how you can effectively use social media to create impactful content and engage with your target audience.

CHOOSING THE RIGHT PLATFORMS

The first step in using social media effectively is selecting the platforms where your audience is most active. Each platform has its strengths and caters to different demographics:

- **Facebook:** Ideal for engaging with homeschool groups, sharing detailed posts, and building a supportive community around your brand.

- **Instagram:** Perfect for showcasing visually appealing content like lesson plans, student projects, or behind-the-scenes glimpses of your homeschool journey.

- **Pinterest:** Excellent for driving traffic to your website or blog by sharing educational resources, curriculum ideas, and printables.

- **YouTube:** Best for offering in-depth content like teaching tutorials, curriculum walkthroughs, or success stories that establish credibility.

- **Likee:** Great for creating short, engaging videos that highlight fun teaching moments, hacks, or creative lesson ideas.

Focus on the platforms that align with your audience and content style, and expand as you gain confidence.

PLANNING AND CREATING CONTENT

Consistency is key when it comes to social media. Planning your content in advance ensures regular posting and keeps your audience engaged. Here's a simple strategy:

- **Educational Content:** Share tips, teaching strategies, or lesson plans that showcase your expertise.

- **Personal Stories:** Talk about your homeschooling journey to connect with your audience on a deeper level.

- **Engaging Questions:** Encourage interaction by asking about their homeschooling challenges or favorite tips.

- **Promotional Posts:** Highlight your services, products, or workshops, but limit these to about 20% of your overall content.

- **Trending Topics:** Stay relevant by incorporating current events or popular themes in the homeschooling space.

EFFICIENT CONTENT CREATION

Save time by batching your content creation. Dedicate time to:

- **Filming Videos:** Record a few videos on homeschool tips or fun activities, and repurpose them into shorter clips for Instagram Reels or TikTok.

- **Designing Graphics:** Use tools like **Canva** to create engaging visuals for platforms like Pinterest and Facebook.

- **Scheduling Posts:** Use tools like **Later** or **Buffer** to plan and schedule posts ahead of time, so you're not tied to your screen daily.

ENGAGING WITH YOUR AUDIENCE

Creating an effective social media presence means building genuine connections, not simply posting. Spend time:

- Responding to comments and messages.

- Participating in homeschool groups or forums to offer advice and share your expertise.

- Asking for feedback to better understand what your audience wants to see.

Engagement creates a sense of community and makes your brand more relatable and trustworthy.

STAYING AUTHENTIC

Your unique perspective as a homeschool parent is your greatest asset. Don't shy away from sharing your real journey, including the ups and downs. Authenticity builds trust and helps your audience see you as a relatable and approachable resource.

EXPERIMENT AND ADAPT

Don't be afraid to experiment with different content types to see what resonates most with your audience, but consistency, quality content, and engagement are key to long-term success. Posting regularly with valuable, relevant content helps build trust and keeps your audience engaged, while actively responding to comments and messages fosters a sense of community. It's important to monitor engagement metrics like likes, shares, and comments to refine your strategy over time, ensuring that your content aligns with what your audience finds most valuable. Social media success is a process, and by consistently delivering meaningful content and engaging authentically, you can grow your presence sustainably. By understanding your audience, maintaining a steady posting schedule, and prioritizing interaction, you can use social media to build a thriving homeschool business that reaches, inspires, and connects with others.

NETWORKING AND MARKETING: IT'S ALL CONNECTED

NETWORKING WITHIN THE HOMESCHOOL COMMUNITY

Networking within the homeschool community is a game-changer for parents looking to turn their passion for homeschooling into a profitable business. Building connections can provide valuable support, resources, and opportunities for collaboration. Here's how you can effectively network and leverage these relationships to grow your business and enrich your homeschooling experience.

1. FIND SUPPORT AND SHARE KNOWLEDGE

Homeschooling can sometimes feel isolating, but connecting with other homeschool parents helps create a sense of community. By engaging with like-minded individuals, you can exchange experiences, challenges, and successes. This mutual support enriches your teaching methods and opens doors for collaboration, such as organizing group activities, co-op classes, or community workshops. These partnerships not only strengthen your homeschooling journey but can also serve as a springboard for business opportunities.

2. ATTEND LOCAL AND NATIONAL EVENTS

Homeschool conventions and events are excellent places to network. These gatherings bring together parents, educators, and vendors, creating a fertile environment for relationship-building.

Workshops and Panels: Attend sessions on homeschooling techniques or entrepreneurial strategies to gain insights and meet potential collaborators.

Vendor Booths: Engage with businesses to explore partnerships or learn about resources that align with your goals.

Face-to-Face Connections: Having in-person conversations helps you establish trust and build lasting relationships that can lead to future collaborations.

3. LEVERAGE ONLINE COMMUNITIES

Online platforms are invaluable for connecting with homeschool families and business owners. Consider joining:

Social Media Groups: Engage with Facebook or Instagram communities focused on homeschooling or education businesses.

Forums and Websites: Participate in discussions on platforms specifically for homeschoolers to exchange curriculum ideas, teaching strategies, or marketing tips.

Sharing Insights: By offering your expertise and actively participating in conversations, you can establish credibility and attract individuals who may be interested in your services or products.

4. Partner with Local Businesses and Institutions

Networking entails connecting with other homeschool families, but local businesses and educational institutions can also play a key role in your success.

Libraries and Museums: Partner with these institutions to offer workshops or classes that complement your business offerings.

Educational Suppliers: Build relationships with curriculum providers or educational vendors to collaborate on resources or sponsorship opportunities.

Community Events: Participate in or host events that allow you to showcase your expertise and connect with potential customers in your area.

5. Focus on Building Authentic Relationships

Networking isn't just about exchanging business cards or social media follows—it's about fostering a supportive community and building meaningful relationships that create mutual opportunities for growth.

- **Be Genuine:** Approach networking with the intention of creating mutually beneficial connections. Whether it's offering advice, sharing resources, or making introductions, always strive to give as much as you receive. Too often, people unknowingly come across as opportunistic by only reaching out when they need something—true networking is about fostering connections built on trust, reciprocity, and shared success. When you approach networking with authenticity and a mindset of service, you'll naturally cultivate relationships that open doors for both you and those around you.

- **Offer Value:** Share your knowledge and insights generously to establish yourself as a trusted resource in the community.

- **Follow Up:** After meeting someone at an event or online, take the time to follow up with a friendly message or idea for collaboration.

Networking within the homeschool community is a powerful tool for turning your passion for education into a thriving business. Whether you're attending events, participating in online groups, or partnering with local businesses, each connection you make adds value to your journey. By actively engaging with others, you'll not only enrich your homeschooling experience but also build a strong foundation for your entrepreneurial success.

Networking and word-of-mouth marketing by parents have been pivotal to the success of Tiers Free Homeschool Cooperative. As families experienced the transformative impact of its trauma-informed curriculum and personalized approach, they naturally became advocates, sharing their stories with others in their communities. This grassroots promotion, fueled by authentic testimonials and trust, allowed Tiers Free to build a strong reputation within homeschool networks and beyond. Networking efforts, such as participating in local events, engaging with online homeschool groups, and fostering collaborative partnerships with other organizations further amplified its reach. By cultivating a supportive community and leveraging the power of parent-driven recommendations, Tiers Free not only grew its enrollment but also solidified its position as a trusted leader in both traditional and nontraditional educational spaces.

 **Chapter 7**

SCALING YOUR HOMESCHOOL BUSINESS FOR LONG-TERM SUCCESS

INTRODUCTION: WHAT SCALING MEANS FOR YOUR HOMESCHOOL BUSINESS

Scaling your homeschool business involves figuring out how to grow without wearing yourself thin, rather than piling on more students or offering a bunch of new things. You want to keep the quality high and stay true to why you started this whole thing in the first place. Think of it like building a house—you need a strong foundation before you can add the fancy second story.

When I built Tiers Free Academy Homeschool Cooperative, I leaned on years of experience working in for-profit education. Every year, l would get anxiety as all of the homeschool moms got together with their beautifully color-coded folders, tabs, and binders as they did a deep dive into planning their homeschool curriculum for the year. But that wasn't me. The truth was I honestly never fit into any of the traditional or non-traditional homeschool spaces.

The one thing I knew for certain was that I wasn't about to create a curriculum from scratch—I wanted to customize something that already existed. Why? Because I knew that I didn't want to build and then perpetually maintain a curriculum; I needed something that worked for me at the moment and had enough flexibility so that in case I got sick, my children wouldn't have to stop learning. Having the ability to easily off-load the task of teaching was key for me in curriculum selection, and especially in how I designed our homeschool cooperative learning schedule. Everything I did could easily be handed off to a fellow adult.

One of the best pieces of advice I ever received came from Jesse Barber, Vice President of The Dr. Annise Mabry Foundation Board of Directors. He told me, "If you don't plan to scale, then you plan to fail." Those words stuck with me. Every time I evaluated a new curriculum vendor, I asked myself, "How easy will this be to scale?" What I didn't realize at the time was that, from the very beginning, I was laying the foundation for growth—intentionally or not.

When it comes to scaling your business, you've got to start by building a solid foundation. Imagine trying to build a house without making sure the ground is level first—everything would crumble the moment you added a second story. The same goes for your business. Before you even think about expansion, you've got to get your ducks in a row.

Tiers Free Homeschool Cooperative's curriculum model serves as a great example of how to develop an effective, scalable educational program. Here's how we structured it to meet the needs of underserved students while maintaining a sustainable business model.

TIERS FREE CASE STUDY: CREATING A SCALABLE HOMESCHOOL COOPERATIVE

OVERVIEW

The Tiers Free Homeschool Cooperative is a pioneering online model based in trauma-informed education that provides tailored academic solutions for students who have been underserved or left behind by traditional systems. By developing a curriculum that bridges skill gaps and aligns with both academic standards and real-world needs, Tiers Free has successfully entered both traditional and nontraditional educational spaces. This dual impact stems from a strategic approach to curriculum development that prioritizes flexibility, inclusivity, and innovation.

The Curriculum Development Strategy

1. Building from the High School Level Down

When Tiers Free was launched, the focus was on high school students who struggled within traditional academic settings. Instead of starting with a broad, general curriculum, the cooperative identified critical gaps in foundational skills among high schoolers.

Process:

- Conducting diagnostic assessments like DORA (Diagnostic Online Reading Assessment) and DOMA (Diagnostic Online Math Assessment) to pinpoint specific deficiencies.

- Developing skill-focused interventions based on high school-level gaps, then adapting these solutions for middle and elementary levels.

- Integrating tools like DreamBox Reading, Reading Eggs, and Exact Path Math to address literacy and numeracy at all grade levels.

2. Trauma-Informed and Individualized Learning

Tiers Free adopted a trauma-informed approach, understanding that many students face challenges beyond academics.

Key Elements:

- Flexible pacing to accommodate students who have fallen behind.

- A blend of online and offline resources tailored to individual learning styles.

- Collaboration with families to create personalized learning plans.

3. Bridging Academic Standards with Real-World Applications

The curriculum balances traditional academic standards with practical life skills and workforce preparation.

Innovations:

- Partnering with programs like DreamBox Reading Plus for evidence-based literacy support.

- Offering workshops on financial literacy, technical skills, and career exploration.

- Selecting online curriculum that meets state and national educational standards to ensure credibility.

WHY THE STRATEGY WORKED

1. Meeting Diverse Needs

Tiers Free's adaptable curriculum uses data-driven assessment tools and aligns with academic standards, making it effective in both traditional settings (like public school collaborations) and nontraditional ones (homeschool families, at-risk youth programs, and alternative education initiatives).

- **Traditional Spaces:** The alignment with academic standards allows seamless partnerships with school districts and educational agencies. For instance, diagnostic assessments provide data-driven insights that schools can use to complement existing interventions.

- **Nontraditional Spaces:** The focus on trauma-informed practices and skill-building makes the curriculum attractive to organizations such as government agencies and community organizations serving homeless LGBTQ youth, human trafficking survivors, and other at-risk populations. Providing the ability for other homeschool networks to purchase site licensing for Tiers Free also expanded the reach and provided resources and expertise to families seeking alternative education solutions.

The curriculum development strategy of Tiers Free Homeschool Cooperative exemplifies how a targeted, inclusive, and adaptable approach can bridge traditional and nontraditional educational spaces. By focusing on skill gaps, aligning with academic standards, and incorporating trauma-informed practices, Tiers Free not only meets the needs of diverse learners but also creates pathways for systemic change in education. This strategy has solidified its role as a transformative force in both conventional and unconventional educational landscapes.

2. Scalability and Flexibility

By using online tools and modular learning plans, Tiers Free created a curriculum that is both scalable and customizable. This flexibility enables the cooperative to:

- Support large-scale implementations in partnership with public schools or agencies.
- Offer individualized learning experiences for smaller homeschool groups or specialized programs.

3. Reputation for Innovation and Results

The cooperative's success in helping over 1,000 students earn diplomas, with 81% securing living-wage jobs and 64% enrolling in technical college programs, has established Tiers Free as a trusted name. This reputation for results makes it an attractive partner in both traditional and nontraditional education sectors.

REVISIT YOUR MISSION AND VISION

First, take a step back and reflect on why you started this journey. Ask yourself, "Does this expansion fit with my mission?" and "How will this growth impact the families I'm serving?" Staying true to your values is nonnegotiable. Growth should add to your brand's identity, not alter it. This clarity will keep you grounded as you scale.

DEVELOP STANDARD OPERATING PROCEDURES (SOPS)

Next, you've got to get organized. I can't stress enough the importance of having clear, step-by-step instructions for everything—from onboarding students to creating lesson plans. These SOPs are lifesavers when you're bringing in help. They ensure everyone is on the same page and that the quality of your services stays consistent, no matter how big you get.

ASSESS YOUR CURRENT RESOURCES

Take a good, hard look at what you've got. Are your tools, team members, and processes working for you, or are they holding you back? If you're drowning in admin work, it might be time to invest in automation tools or hire a virtual assistant. Scaling is a team effort, and knowing your limits is key.

DIVERSIFYING YOUR OFFERINGS

If you want to grow, you've got to think beyond your current services. The more ways you can help homeschool families, the more opportunities you'll create for your business.

EXPAND SERVICES

- Consider adding:
- One-on-one tutoring for tough subjects.
- Workshops or webinars for parents navigating homeschooling challenges.
- Mentorship programs for those just starting out.

CREATE PASSIVE INCOME STREAMS

This is where things get exciting. Passive income allows you to generate revenue even when you're not actively working, giving you both financial stability and freedom. Think about writing e-books on homeschooling hacks, recording on-demand courses that families can purchase and watch anytime, or offering subscription-based lesson plans tailored to different grade levels.

For Tiers Free Homeschool Cooperative, I built passive income streams by partnering with curriculum vendors, creating digital resources that could be reused year after year, and developing a structured homeschool diploma program that families could follow independently. By leveraging affiliate partnerships, downloadable educational resources, and automated enrollment processes, I ensured that Tiers Free could scale sustainably without requiring constant hands-on involvement. These strategies not only increased revenue but also freed up my time, allowing me to focus on expanding our impact and supporting more students.

FRANCHISING OR LICENSING

When Tiers Free began to scale, I had to decide—do I let people borrow my model (licensing), or do I create a full system they could replicate step by step (franchising)? Understanding this difference early on helped me make smart business decisions while keeping control over my brand.

If your homeschool model is working well, you might be wondering how to share it with others while also generating income. Franchising and licensing are two ways to do this, but they work differently.

Licensing – Think of licensing like giving someone permission to use your homeschool curriculum, lesson plans, or teaching methods for a fee. You still own the materials, but you allow others to use them under specific rules. For example, you could license your homeschool curriculum to other parents or co-ops, so they follow your system but still operate independently.

Franchising – This is more structured. Instead of just giving permission to use materials, franchising allows someone to replicate your entire homeschool model, including branding, operations, and curriculum—kind of like opening a new location of a well-known restaurant. If you franchise your homeschool cooperative, another parent or educator would run their own version of it, following your established guidelines and branding, while paying a fee or percentage of earnings.

Both options let you expand your impact without doing all the hands-on work yourself—licensing is more flexible, while franchising requires more control but offers bigger growth potential.

If your model is working like a charm, why not let others use it?

LEVERAGING TECHNOLOGY FOR SCALE

Technology is your best friend when it comes to scaling without losing your mind.

Invest in Learning Management Systems (LMS)

A good LMS, like Google Classroom, Moodle, or Thinkific can simplify everything from delivering courses to tracking progress. It's a game-changer, especially when you are ready to create passive income.

When I realized that my knowledge of both homeschool law and grant writing had value, I turned it into a passive income centered business by creating on-demand courses on the Thinkific platform. What I like about Thinkific is I can sell individual courses, memberships, or digital resources. This allows me to generate a passive income for the nonprofit and I am still helping other families.

Automate Repetitive Tasks

Save yourself time and energy with tools like Mailchimp for newsletters, scheduling apps for meetings or classes, and chatbots to answer FAQs on your website. These small changes can make a huge difference.

Expand Your Online Presence

Going virtual allows you to connect with families all over the world. Platforms like Zoom and YouTube make it easier than ever to offer virtual classes and e-learning resources.

BUILDING STRATEGIC PARTNERSHIPS

You can't do this alone, and you shouldn't have to. Strategic partnerships are a way to grow faster, but moreover, they are essential for sustainability and impact. The right partnerships allow you to scale efficiently, leverage shared resources, and expand your reach without carrying the full burden yourself. Aligning with trusted organizations, businesses, and education leaders strengthens credibility, opens doors to funding opportunities, and enhances the value you provide to families.

For example, partnering with curriculum vendors, learning management systems, and local workforce development programs enables homeschool cooperatives to offer more robust services without reinventing the wheel. Collaborations with nonprofits and grant programs can provide financial support, scholarships, and essential resources to ensure long-term sustainability. Meanwhile, engaging with businesses and community organizations creates internship, mentorship, and job-shadowing opportunities, helping students transition from education to employment.

The most effective partnerships are built on mutual benefit. Beyond focusing on individual success, a thriving homeschool model aims to build an ecosystem of support that benefits families, educators, and communities as a whole.

COLLABORATE WITH LOCAL ORGANIZATIONS AND HOMESCHOOL NETWORKS

Team up with libraries, community centers, or nonprofits. Get involved in homeschool groups and co-ops. These connections can lead to new clients and collaborations. For instance, you could host free workshops at a library to show off your expertise or partner with a community center to serve underserved families.

CORPORATE SPONSORSHIPS AND GRANTS

Look for companies or organizations that align with your mission. Sponsorships and grants can provide the funding you need to take your business to the next level.

GROWING YOUR TEAM

Scaling your homeschool business can feel like a big leap, but with the right steps, it's totally doable. Start small, stay focused on your mission, and build a business that grows with you. The key is to make thoughtful decisions that help you grow without losing what makes your business special. You've got this!

HOW I MANAGE GROWTH, TIME, AND TEAM BUILDING

For me, time management isn't about working harder—it's about working smarter. Scaling Tiers Free Homeschool Cooperative, keeping our programs sustainable, and maintaining high-quality educational services means I have to be intentional about delegation, financial planning, and strategic growth. Here's how I make it all work—without burning out or losing sight of my mission.

KNOWING WHEN TO HIRE: SCALING WITHOUT CHAOS

I knew it was time to grow my team when demand for Tiers Free outpaced what I could handle alone. Instead of waiting until I was completely overwhelmed, I made a list of tasks that only I could do and another list of tasks that someone else could handle with the right training. That's when I started bringing in virtual assistants to handle admin work, subject matter experts to strengthen my courses, and marketing professionals to help me expand my reach. By letting go of tasks that didn't need my direct attention, I freed up my time to focus on growth, strategy, and impact—the things that actually move my business forward.

FINANCIAL GROWTH: BUDGETING FOR SMART EXPANSION

Scaling takes not only time, but money, and I don't believe in wasting a single dollar. I budget carefully for new tools, additional staff, and marketing, but I also keep a close eye on cash flow so I never overextend myself. I don't rely on merely one funding source—I leverage grants, partnerships, and strategic investments to fuel expansion without putting my organization at financial risk. Every decision I make is an investment in long-term sustainability, not just short-term growth.

MARKETING TO A LARGER AUDIENCE
WITHOUT LOSING MY MISSION

As Tiers Free grew, I had to be intentional about my marketing. I didn't want to simply throw money at ads and hope for the best; I needed to make sure I was reaching the right families who actually needed my programs. So, I refined my messaging, highlighted real success stories, and used data-driven marketing strategies to expand my reach. I made sure that no matter how much we grew, our message stayed clear: Tiers Free exists to serve at-risk students who have been left behind by traditional education systems.

AVOIDING COMMON PITFALLS:
SCALING WITH PURPOSE

Growth isn't the goal—impact is. I've seen too many people scale too fast, lose their core mission, and then struggle to maintain quality. I refused to let that happen. I paced my expansion to avoid burnout, consistently checked in to ensure my students were getting the best education possible, and stayed true to what makes Tiers Free different. I didn't chase trends or try to compete with big education companies—I stayed focused on what I do best: providing trauma-informed, flexible educational solutions for underserved students.

THE KEY TO SUSTAINABLE GROWTH

Scaling is about making smart, strategic decisions that let my business grow with me, not against me. By building the right team, managing my finances wisely, and staying true to my mission, I've created a thriving homeschool business that continues to grow without sacrificing quality. The lesson? You don't have to do it all—you just have to do it right.

 **Chapter 8**

OVERCOMING CHALLENGES AS A HOMESCHOOL ENTREPRENEUR

The journey of turning your passion for homeschooling into a thriving business is one of the most rewarding things you'll ever do—but let me tell you, it is not without its challenges. From managing your time to dealing with criticism from naysayers, you'll encounter bumps along the way. What sets successful entrepreneurs apart isn't avoiding obstacles—it's learning how to face them head-on and keep going. Let's dive into some of the challenges you might face and how to overcome them.

NAVIGATING BURNOUT AND TIME MANAGEMENT

When I first started homeschooling and running a business, I felt like I was spinning a million plates at once. Between teaching my kids, running Tiers Free Academy, and just trying to keep my head above water, burnout felt like it was always lurking around the corner. It's something every entrepreneur faces, but here's what I've learned about keeping it at bay.

PRIORITIZE SELF-CARE

You can't pour from an empty cup. I used to hear that all the time and roll my eyes, but it's true. You've got to make time for yourself—even if it's only fifteen minutes of peace with a cup of coffee in the morning. Find what rejuvenates you. For me, it's reading a good book or taking a quiet walk. For you, it might be something else. Whatever it is, make it nonnegotiable.

TIME-BLOCKING AND SCHEDULING

I'll let you in on a little secret—time-blocking saved my sanity. I block out my mornings for homeschooling and my afternoons for business tasks. It's all about being intentional with your time. Tools like Google Calendar became my best friends. Seeing my day planned out helped me stay focused and kept the overwhelm at bay.

DELEGATE AND OUTSOURCE

One of the biggest lessons I've learned is that I don't have to do everything myself. I've hired virtual assistants for admin tasks and leaned on co-op resources when homeschooling felt like too much. Delegation isn't a weakness—it's smart business.

SET BOUNDARIES

I used to let my work bleed into every part of my life. I'd answer emails at the dinner table or take calls during family time. That's a recipe for burnout. Now, I set boundaries. My family knows when I'm working, and my clients know when I'm not available. It's about protecting your time and energy.

HANDLING CRITICISM FROM TRADITIONAL EDUCATION ADVOCATES

Let's be real—not everyone will understand or support what you're doing as a homeschool entrepreneur. I've faced my fair share of skeptics who questioned the legitimacy of homeschooling or doubted whether my business was "real" education. Here's how I handle it.

RESPOND WITH CONFIDENCE

When someone questions your work, don't get defensive. Instead, lean on your results. I've always said that success speaks louder than words. Share your students' successes, highlight their growth, and let your results do the talking.

STAY PROFESSIONAL

I've learned to stay calm and composed, even when the criticism feels personal. Taking the high road not only protects your reputation but also shows that you're serious about what you do.

FOCUS ON YOUR IMPACT

I don't waste energy trying to convince everyone. Instead, I focus on the families I'm helping. Their positive experiences and testimonials are the best response to critics.

JOIN ADVOCACY NETWORKS

There's power in numbers. Being part of homeschool advocacy groups has given me resources and strategies to address criticism effectively. Plus, it's empowering to know you're not alone.

LESSONS LEARNED FROM FAILURES AND HOW TO PIVOT EFFECTIVELY

Here's the thing about failure—it's not the end. It's just a step in the process. I've made mistakes along the way, but each one taught me something valuable. Let me share what I've learned about bouncing back.

EMBRACE A GROWTH MINDSET

Every failure is a lesson in disguise. When something doesn't work, I ask myself, "What can I learn from this? How can I do better next time?" It's about seeing failures as stepping stones, not roadblocks.

ANALYZE AND ADAPT

Take a moment to figure out what went wrong. Maybe a new service didn't resonate with your audience. Was it the timing? The way you marketed it? Once you know, you can pivot. When I realized one of my programs wasn't meeting families' needs, I reworked it until it did. Don't be afraid to adjust your approach.

CELEBRATE SMALL WINS

It's easy to focus on what's not working, but don't forget to celebrate what is. Whether it's a positive email from a client or hitting a small milestone, those wins keep you motivated.

SEEK MENTORSHIP

I can't emphasize enough how much mentorship has helped me. Learning from others who've been there can save you time and heartache. Don't be afraid to reach out and ask for advice.

Challenges are part of the journey, but they don't have to define your story. By managing your time wisely, staying confident in the face of criticism, and embracing failures as learning opportunities, you can overcome anything that comes your way. Remember, every challenge you conquer not only makes you stronger but also inspires others. Keep your eyes on your mission, stay true to your values, and trust that you've got what it takes to succeed.

 **Chapter 9**

INNOVATING IN THE HOMESCHOOL SPACE

Homeschooling is an ever-evolving journey, and as entrepreneurs in this space, we must be ready to adapt, innovate, and embrace change. The educational landscape is shifting faster than ever, with new trends like micro-schools, hybrid learning, and advancements in technology reshaping how we approach education. Let's dive into these exciting developments and explore how staying ahead of the curve can help you build a homeschool business that thrives.

EXPLORING NEW TRENDS IN EDUCATION

Micro-schools are changing the game in education, and honestly, I wish they had been around when I first started homeschooling. Think of them as a blend between homeschooling and traditional school—but on a much smaller, more personalized scale. These schools typically serve 10-15 students, offering customized learning, small group instruction, and hands-on, real-world projects that actually engage kids.

Here's why I love them: micro-schools give kids the flexibility of homeschooling but with the social and academic structure of a traditional school. They're perfect for families who want more control over their child's education but don't want to go it alone. If you've ever thought about starting a homeschool collective, co-op, or small learning pod, a micro-school could be your next step.

Getting started is easier than you think. The key is finding like-minded families who share your educational values, as well as building a learning environment that fits your community's needs. Whether you focus on STEM, entrepreneurship, project-based learning, or trauma-informed education, a micro-school gives you the freedom to create the kind of school you always wished existed.

HYBRID LEARNING: THE BEST OF BOTH WORLDS

Hybrid learning combines in-person instruction with online resources, giving students the flexibility to learn at their own pace while still benefiting from face-to-face interaction. This model has exploded in popularity since the pandemic and is a fantastic option for homeschool families who want more structure without sacrificing flexibility.

As a homeschool entrepreneur, consider offering hybrid learning options. You might create a program where students attend classes a few days a week and complete assignments online the rest of the time. Tools like Zoom, Google Classroom, and interactive learning platforms make it easier than ever to implement hybrid models.

SPECIALIZED LEARNING PODS

Learning pods are small groups of students who study together, often facilitated by a tutor or educator. What makes learning pods unique is their ability to focus on specific needs, whether it's advanced STEM education, art enrichment, or addressing learning gaps. As an entrepreneur, you can carve out a niche by creating and managing specialized pods that cater to unique interests or challenges within your community.

STAYING AHEAD OF CHANGES IN TECHNOLOGY AND HOMESCHOOLING LAWS

LEVERAGING TECHNOLOGY FOR INNOVATION

Technology is transforming homeschooling in ways we couldn't have imagined a decade ago. From virtual reality (VR) field trips to AI-driven tutoring, the possibilities are endless. Staying informed about these advancements can set your business apart. For instance:

- **VR and AR Learning:** Offer immersive learning experiences that bring history, science, and geography to life.

- **AI-Powered Tools:** Use platforms like DreamBox or Khan Academy, which adapt to students' learning levels in real-time.

- **Gamification:** Engage students with educational games that make learning fun and interactive.

KEEPING UP WITH HOMESCHOOLING LAWS

Homeschooling laws vary by state and are constantly evolving. Staying compliant means more than merely following the rules; it means protecting your business and the families you serve. I make it a habit to check state regulations regularly and encourage other entrepreneurs to do the same. Consider joining organizations like the Home School Legal Defense Association (HSLDA) to stay informed and access legal resources.

By embracing new trends and staying proactive about changes in the homeschool space, you position yourself as a forward-thinking leader who can offer innovative, compliant, and effective solutions for families.

Dr. Annise Mabry

# Chapter 10

SUCCESS STORIES AND INSPIRATION

Sometimes, the best motivation comes from hearing about others who have walked this path and come out on top. I have seen firsthand how homeschool businesses can reshape futures, restore confidence, and open doors that traditional education often slams shut. I want to share with you real stories of people who took their passion for education and turned it into a business, making a lasting impact on their communities.

HOMESCHOOL BUSINESSES THAT THRIVED

TIERS FREE ACADEMY HOMESCHOOL COOPERATIVE

When I started Tiers Free Academy, I had no idea how far it would go. What began as a small program to help at-risk high school students has grown into a six-figure nonprofit that has issued over 1,000 diplomas to students who had been written off by the traditional school system.

The key to our success? We meet students where they are. Instead of forcing them to fit into a broken system, we designed education to fit them. We use trauma-informed, personalized learning that focuses on what students need to graduate and thrive, not just what a standardized test says they should know.

One of my favorite success stories is about a young man who came to us after being expelled from multiple schools. He was labeled a problem student, but I knew he wasn't the problem—it was the system that had failed him. He struggled with reading and had almost given up on earning a diploma. With the right support, patience, and a customized learning plan, he not only graduated but also completed a technical certification in welding. Today, he is working a full-time job in his trade, making good money, and building a future for himself. That's why I do this work.

TIERS FREE TESTIMONIALS FROM FAMILIES AND STUDENTS

TRANSFORMATIVE IMPACT ON FAMILIES

Beyond providing alternatives to traditional education, homeschooling is a way to restore confidence. I once had a mother reach out to me in tears because her bright, capable daughter was struggling in school. Teachers told her she wasn't trying hard enough. The truth? She wasn't being taught in a way that worked for her.

After enrolling in Tiers Free Academy, she discovered a love for science, and for the first time in years, she believed she was smart. Today, she's studying environmental science and on track to pursue a career in conservation. Her mom told me, "You gave us hope when we didn't think we had any left."

That's why we do this—to give families a new vision of what education can be.

EMPOWERING STUDENTS TO SUCCEED AGAINST ALL ODDS

I'll never forget one young man who came to us while he was homeless. Sleeping in a tent and bouncing from couch to couch, he had already lost faith in the idea of finishing high school.

We enrolled him in Tiers Free Academy, and for the first time, he had a path forward. Not only did we give him coursework, but we also provided him with life skills, connected him with mentors, and helped him see his own potential.

A year later, he graduated. That diploma wasn't just a piece of paper—it was proof that he was more than his circumstances.

A few months after that, I got a message from him. It said: "Thank you for believing in me when no one else did."

That's the power of homeschool education.

SPECIALIZED TUTORING BUSINESSES

I've seen so many homeschool parents turn their expertise into thriving tutoring businesses, simply by identifying a need and filling the gap.

One parent I worked with had a gift for teaching math. She wasn't just good at it—she had a way of explaining things that actually made sense to kids who struggled with numbers. She started small, offering one-on-one tutoring to a few local families. But she didn't stop there. She figured out a way to incorporate real-world applications into her lessons by showing kids how math is used in construction, business, and even everyday tasks like budgeting.

Word spread fast. Within a year, she had hired two additional tutors, launched online math workshops, and was working with students across the country. What started as a side hustle became a full-time business—all because she recognized a need, built a system that worked, and wasn't afraid to take the leap.

FROM HOMESCHOOLER TO PUBLISHER: A STORY OF REINVENTION AND RESILIENCE

By Aimee Andrichak

Being a single mother, just finishing up a messy divorce, sharing custody of my four oldest children, and having a small child to care for was more difficult than anything else I had ever faced. The emotional toll of rebuilding my life while ensuring my children felt stable and loved was overwhelming. Finances were tight, and every decision felt like it carried immense weight. I had to find a way to support my family while still being present for my children.

I worked as a live-in nanny and homeschool educator for a while, homeschooling my client's children while also assisting with household chores, errands, and anything else that needed to be done. It was exhausting but also rewarding, as I found joy in teaching and creating a nurturing environment. However, I knew that this wasn't my long-term path. I wanted something of my own, something that would allow me to use my creativity and skills to build a sustainable future for my family.

I had always dreamed of being a writer. Since childhood, I had filled journals with stories, recipes, and ideas, but life had always seemed to get in the way. During my previous marriage, I had taken a step toward that dream by publishing my own cookbook. It was a small, self-published project, but it gave me valuable experience in the world of independent publishing. I learned about formatting, cover design, marketing, and distribution—skills that would later prove invaluable.

When I started my tiny publishing company, I was living in the basement of a dear friend's house. She had opened her home to me in my time of need, and in return, I helped educate her children while caring for my newborn baby. It was a challenging period, filled with long nights and uncertain days, but it was also a time of clarity. I realized that if I could publish my own book, I could help others do the same.

At first, it was just an idea, something I toyed with between changing diapers and preparing lessons. But then, people started reaching out—friends, acquaintances, even strangers—asking how I had self-published my cookbook. They had stories to tell, recipes to share, and knowledge they wanted to put into print but didn't know where to begin. I found myself answering questions, offering guidance, and before long, taking on small projects to help others bring their books to life.

What started as a necessity quickly became a passion. I threw myself into learning everything I could about the publishing industry, refining my process, and building connections with printers, editors, and designers. My tiny publishing company was born out of a mix of desperation and determination, but it grew because I genuinely loved what I was doing—helping others bring their ideas to life and hold their own books in their hands.

Looking back, I see those early days as the foundation of something greater than I ever imagined. What began as a way to survive became a career, a calling, and a testament to the power of resilience and reinvention.

When I originally self-published my first cookbook, it was out of joy more than necessity. As a homeschool mom, I took it on as a passion project, wanting to show my kids that they are never too old to chase their dreams. I wanted them to see first-hand that learning doesn't stop with childhood and that creative endeavors are always worth pursuing. It was a whirlwind, but when I finally held that first copy in my hands, I knew I had done something special. It was proof that dedication and perseverance could turn an idea into something tangible, something real.

Unfortunately, just after I published that first book, my life hit a stumbling block. The dissolution of my marriage left me struggling to figure out how to care for my children while still pursuing my dreams. I knew I had skills and ambition, but finding a way to translate that into financial stability was another challenge altogether. Slowly, I started building up my publishing business in whatever ways I could. I wrote website copy for a shoe company. I edited, proofread, beta read, and touched up doctoral theses, websites, books, and business plans. If it was made of words, I would help refine it. Bit by bit, I built up a group of clients who believed in me and my vision, trusting me with their work.

All the while, I continued working as a home educator, teaching homeschool classes for local co-ops and educating my own young children. It was an exhausting time, balancing so many responsibilities, but I was determined to make it work. My love for writing and storytelling never wavered, even in the most difficult moments.

Life became much easier after I married my wonderful husband. With him, I had a support system, a home of my own, and most importantly, someone to share my dreams with. His encouragement helped me to push forward and take my business to the next level.

Inspired, I wrote and self-published many more cookbooks, refining my process each time. By the third book, I had a system in place and a deep understanding of how to navigate the tricky waters of independent publishing. I became faster, more efficient, and more confident in my abilities.

That's when the clients really started coming in.

At first, I gave advice freely, sharing my experiences over coffee or long email exchanges. But as the requests increased, I realized there was a real demand for publishing guidance, especially from people who didn't want to go through the traditional route. That's when the idea struck me—why not turn my tiny self-publishing house into a real business?

I started small, helping a friend format her book on traditional herbal practices. Then another client came along, an artisanal bread maker with a stunning collection of recipes and stories.

With each project, I refined my services—editing, layout, cover design, and marketing strategy. The more books I helped publish, the more I realized that this wasn't just a side project. It was a career shift. While I loved teaching and homeschooling more than any other job I had ever had, I knew that I had a chance to truly reach for the golden ring, and I was going to take it.

Within a year, I discovered the world of ghostwriting. Many of my clients were speakers, coaches, and leaders in their fields who needed content to promote themselves and share their visions. Unfortunately, not everyone with a great story to tell has the time or ability to translate it onto paper. That's where I found my niche.

Through ghostwriting, I get to live the lives of so many people. I interview them, dive into their experiences, and help them share their stories with the world in their own voice. It is an honor, and it inspires me to get out of bed in the morning and fire up my laptop. Every book I help create is a collaboration, a labor of love that brings someone's unique perspective into the world.

Word spread quickly, and soon, I had a full roster of clients. The projects were diverse—cookbooks, memoirs, self-help guides, business books, and more. Each book was an opportunity to bring a dream to life, and helping authors see their work in print became one of my greatest delights.

Looking back, I never would have guessed that self-publishing my first cookbook as a homeschool project with my kids would lead to starting my own publishing company. But sometimes, the best opportunities come from simply following a passion and being open to where it leads. What started as a personal venture became a thriving business, proving that there's always room at the table for more stories to be told—and that with determination, resilience, and a little bit of faith, the most delicious dreams can come true.

WHY THESE STORIES MATTER

The homeschool community is filled with innovators, dreamers, and changemakers—people who refuse to accept "this is just how things are" and instead ask, "How can we make this better?"

By staying open to new trends, leveraging technology, and learning from those who have succeeded, we can continue to redefine education and change lives. Remember, your homeschool business is more than a method of generating income—it is a chance to create opportunities, break down barriers, and give students and families the future they deserve.

Let these stories fuel your passion. If they did it, you can too. Now, go build something amazing.

 # Chapter 11

CREATING IMPACT BEYOND PROFIT

When I first started my homeschool journey, my focus was solely on my family—getting my kids through tough times and ensuring they had the education they deserved. But as Tiers Free Academy grew, I realized something powerful: this work could be so much more than simply a business. It could be a way to transform lives and create lasting change in our communities. That's the heart of this chapter—how to use your homeschool business to make an impact that goes far beyond profit.

BUILDING COMMUNITY PROGRAMS OR COOPERATIVES

There is nothing like the magic that happens when people come together for a common purpose. Community programs and cooperatives are vehicles not only for pooling resources, but also for building connections and creating spaces where families feel supported and valued.

START SMALL AND STAY FOCUSED

When I launched Tiers Free Academy, it started with one goal: help my oldest child get a high school diploma. Once my child graduated, my focus shifted to other high school students who were struggling. Over time, it grew into a cooperative that served K-12, but it didn't happen overnight. My advice? Start small. Focus on one specific group or need—whether it's tutoring, extracurricular activities, or diploma pathways. When you're clear about your mission, everything else falls into place.

ENGAGE FAMILIES AS PARTNERS

One of the things that makes cooperatives so special is the sense of ownership they create. When families have a voice in the program—whether it's through decision-making, volunteering, or contributing ideas—they're more invested in its success. Don't simply run the show; invite families to be part of it.

LEVERAGE LOCAL RESOURCES

You'd be amazed at what's available in your community when you start asking. Libraries, community centers, and even local businesses are often eager to support educational initiatives. Partnering with these organizations can provide space, funding, or resources that make a big difference without breaking your budget.

GIVING BACK TO UNDERSERVED COMMUNITIES

If there's one thing I've learned, it's that education can be a lifeline for families who feel like they've run out of options. Giving back isn't just about charity—it's about equity and empowerment.

IDENTIFY THE GAPS

Every community has unique needs. Maybe it's families who can't afford traditional homeschooling materials, or maybe it's students who've been overlooked in public school settings. Take the time to understand what's missing and where you can step in to make a difference.

OFFER SCHOLARSHIPS OR FREE RESOURCES

One example of how Tiers Free Academy gives back is by offering scholarships for families who can't afford tuition. We have some amazing corporate partnerships with companies like the International Paper

Foundation, State Farm Communities Foundation, Walmart Communities Foundation, General Mills Foundation, Tegan and Sara Foundation, and the Dollar General Literacy Foundation. All of these partnerships have made it possible for me to take this program into rural communities all over Georgia and transform not only their graduation rates but also their early literacy fluency in reading and math. Even if your business is just getting off the ground, there are ways to provide support—whether it's free workshops, donated curriculum, or sliding-scale pricing.

COLLABORATE WITH NONPROFITS

Partnering with organizations that already serve underserved populations can amplify your impact. For example, we've worked with nonprofits focused on LGBTQ+ youth and human trafficking survivors to provide diploma pathways. These partnerships allow us to reach people who might never have found us on their own.

ALIGNING BUSINESS GOALS WITH SOCIAL GOOD

Making a difference doesn't have to be separate from running a successful business. In fact, the two can go hand-in-hand. When you align your goals with a mission that serves others, you create a business that's not only profitable but also deeply fulfilling.

DEFINE YOUR CORE VALUES

Start by getting clear on what matters most to you. For me, it's equity, accessibility, and second chances. These values guide every decision I make, from the programs we offer to the partners we work with. Your values will become the foundation of your brand and the reason families choose you over someone else.

BE TRANSPARENT ABOUT YOUR MISSION

Families want to know that their money is supporting something meaningful. Share your mission openly on your website, in newsletters, or through social media. Let people see the impact of their investment in real-time, through success stories, photos, and updates.

Measure Your Impact

It's one thing to say you're making a difference, but it's another to show it. Track metrics that matter to your mission: the number of students you've served, diplomas issued, or families supported. These numbers not only demonstrate your success but also inspire others to support your work.

 # Chapter 12

EMBRACING THE ENTREPRENEURIAL JOURNEY

As we come to the end of this book, I want to take a moment to reflect on the incredible journey you're about to embark on. Starting a homeschool business means you are following a passion and creating something extraordinary. You are taking the challenges you've faced, the lessons you've learned, and the dreams you've nurtured, and turning them into a legacy that impacts not only your family but countless others.

YOUR POWER TO TRANSFORM LIVES

If there's one thing I've learned, it's that homeschooling has the power to change lives in ways we can't always predict. When I started Tiers Free Academy, I never imagined it would grow into what it is today. But every step of the way, I reminded myself of one simple truth: this work matters. Every diploma earned, every student who discovered their potential, every family that found hope—those are the moments that define success.

And now, it's your turn. You have the power to create that kind of impact. You're not just building a business; you're shaping futures, building communities, and transforming education. That's a responsibility, yes, but it's also an incredible privilege.

FACING THE CHALLENGES

Let's be honest—this road isn't always smooth. There will be days when you question yourself, when the weight of responsibility feels overwhelming, or when you're faced with obstacles you didn't see coming. But those moments aren't the end of your story. They're the beginning of something new.

The setbacks will teach you resilience. The challenges will force you to grow. And every time you pick yourself up and keep going, you're proving to yourself and the world that you're capable of incredible things. Remember, failure isn't the opposite of success—it's part of the journey.

DREAM BIG, START SMALL

It's easy to get caught up in the big picture, but don't underestimate the power of starting small. Maybe your business begins with just a few families or a single program. That's okay. Every great endeavor starts with a single step. Focus on doing what you do best, and let your passion guide you. As you grow, the impact will come naturally.

When I started my work, I wasn't thinking about creating a six-figure nonprofit. I was thinking about the one student in front of me, the one family who needed hope. And that focus on the individual—on meeting people where they are—is what built the foundation for everything that followed.

YOU'RE NOT ALONE

One of the most beautiful things about this journey is the community you'll find along the way. Homeschooling can sometimes feel isolating, but as an entrepreneur, you're joining a network of dreamers and doers who are just as passionate as you are about reshaping education. Lean on that community. Share your struggles, celebrate your victories, and collaborate whenever you can.

And remember, you have a seat at the table. Your voice, your experiences, and your vision matter. Together, we are more than individuals running businesses; we are part of a movement that's redefining what education can look like.

TRANSFORMING LIVES, INCLUDING YOUR OWN

What I love most about this journey is that the transformation isn't just for the families you serve. It's for you, too. Building a homeschool business will challenge you in ways you've never imagined. It will push you to grow, to learn, and to become the best version of yourself. And along the way, you'll discover strengths you didn't know you had.

As you move forward, don't forget to celebrate your progress. Every milestone—no matter how small—is worth acknowledging. You're doing a remarkable thing, and that deserves to be celebrated.

FINAL THOUGHTS

If there's one thing I want you to take away from this book, it's that you have the power to create something extraordinary. Homeschooling is more than educating your kids—it's also reimagining what education can be. And when you turn that passion into a business, you are building not only a career, but also a lasting legacy.

The road won't always be easy. There will be challenges, setbacks, and moments when you wonder if it's all worth it. But let me tell you—it is. Every family you help, every student you inspire, every life you touch—that's your impact. And it's bigger than any paycheck or profit margin.

Dream big. Be bold. And know that this journey isn't yours alone. You're part of a community of changemakers who are reshaping education, one family at a time. Together, we're not just teaching—we're transforming lives.

www.ingramcontent.com/pod-product-compliance
Lightning Source LLC
Chambersburg PA
CBHW031226120626
46545CB00003B/1010